Bang!

Written by
Daisy Hawkins

Illustrated by
Nicolas Rix

ished in 2026 by
wood House Press
4 Clinton Street
alo, NY 14224

ed in the United States of America

Library of Congress Cataloging-in-Publication Data:
Names: Hawkins, Daisy, author. | Serafin, Miriam, illustrator. | Rix, Nicolas, illustrator.
Title: Bang! / written by Daisy Hawkins, illustrated by Nicolas Rix. Hair art / written by Daisy Hawkins.
Description: Buffalo, NY : Norwood House Press, 2026. | Series: Phonics all-stars: phase 3 |
Identifiers: ISBN 9781978577909 (pbk.) | ISBN 9781978577916 (library bound) | ISBN 9781978577923 (ebook)
Subjects: LCSH: Reading–Phonetic method–Juvenile literature. | English language–Phonetics–Juvenile literature. | Superheroes–Juvenile literature. | Hairstyles–Juvenile literature. | Hair–Juvenile literature.
Classification: LCC LB1573.3 H395 2026 | DDC 372.465–dc2

CPSIA compliance information: Batch #CW26NHP: For further information contact Norwood House Press at 1-800-237-9932.

In a boring park in a boring, dull town, Tim is on the job ...
That cat is high up.
Is it sick? Can it get down?

Tim will get it ...
Bang!
Um ... Good job, Tim.

In a shop, in a town that is a bit less boring ...
Get that man! He took my bag!

Quick, Tim! We need you.
Bang!
Um ... Good job, Tim.

High, high up, in the cockpit of a jet ...
Right, Jeff, can you get this jet down?
Wait, Jeff? Are you with me? Are you ill?

This might be bad ...
Bang!
Um ... Good job, Tim.

In a town in Japan ...
Look at it boiling up!
The town is in peril. We all need to go right now!

Are you getting that bad feeling yet?

On a ship far, far off ...
Coil the red cord up tight. Then join it to this bit.
They are in for such a shock!

Not now, Tim ...
Bang!

OK, Tim. That was **not** such a good job.

Hair Art

By Daisy Hawkins

Hair can be a form of art.

You can go for all sorts of "looks."

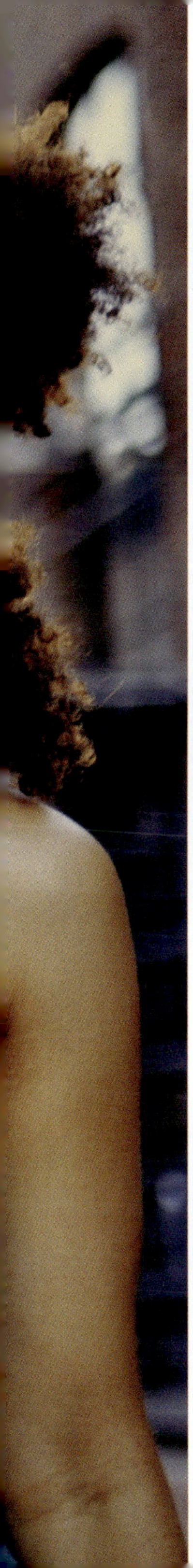

She has a lob (that is, a long bob).

She has highlights too.

Highlights look good with a lob, but the foils are not a quick job!

She has a bun.

You might need to pop pins in a bun, to keep it high and tight.

Hair is not near the ears in this look.

Or you can part the hair and get lots of buns.

He has a quiff.

Forget pins! You need to set a quiff with hair wax.

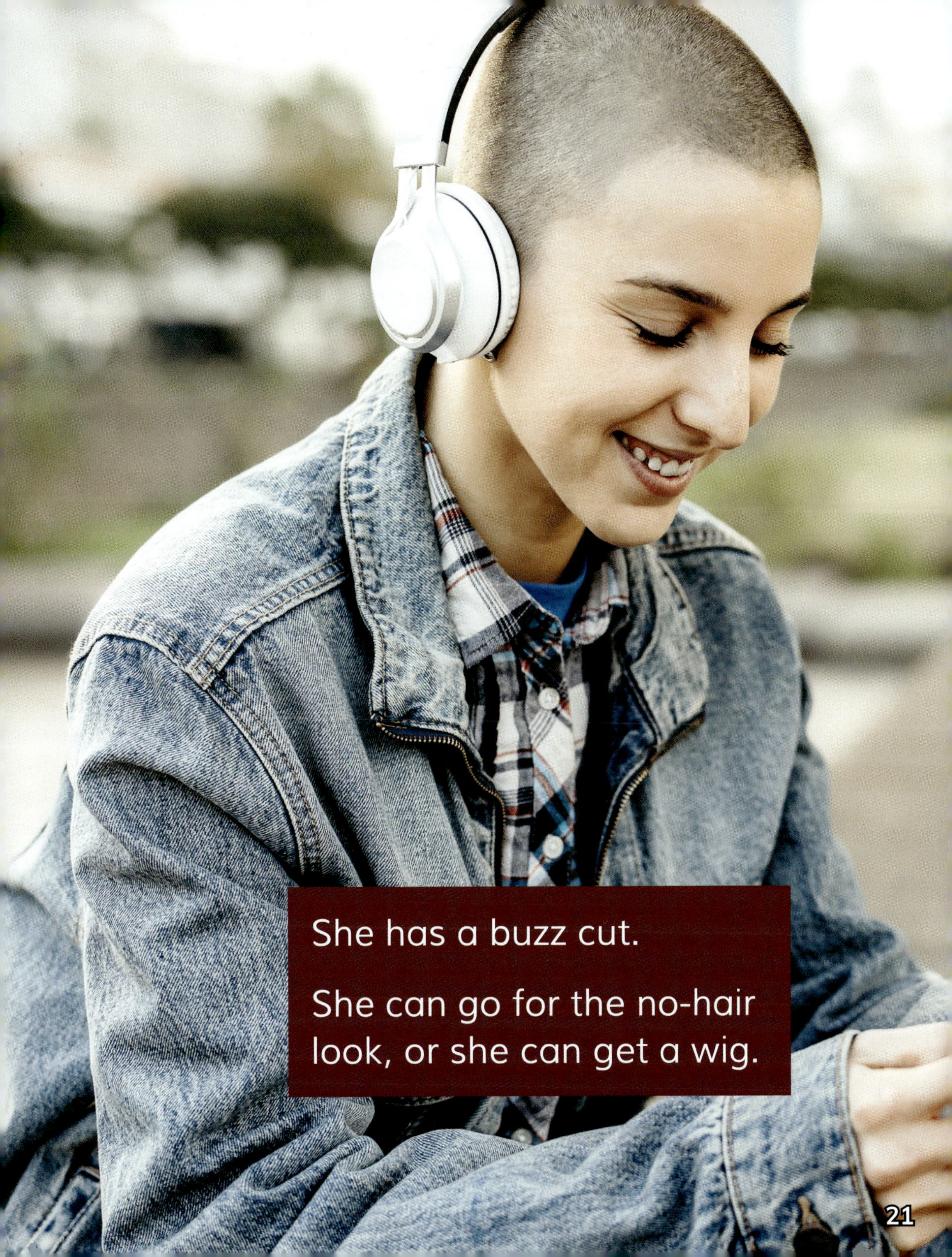

She has a buzz cut.

She can go for the no-hair look, or she can get a wig.

Wigs are good if you want to try long hair, short hair, fair hair, **and** dark hair.

With a wig, you can get a look for a bit, then go back to how it was.

He has a beard. Beard hair can be part of a look too.

For a sharp beard, you need to keep the chin high as you cut it.

Beards need shampoo and oil too.

Now that you are in my chair, will you go for hair that is art?